Shipboard

Luigi steps out from behind a crate on the Doom Ship's deck. " " he says. "Right now, the Mushroom King is a giant rabbit. And the Koopas did it to him!"

"Tough!" snaps Iggy Koopa. He gives the Doom Ship's steering wheel a swift spin. Then he scampers to the railing and jumps. "Ta-ta," he laughs.

Iggy's white canvas backpack opens and a small parachute pops out. The turtle drifts through the clouds and disappears. Then the ship begins to spin violently out of control.

"Yikes!" Luigi lunges for the steering wheel. But it's too late. The boat flips sideways, then upside down, then rightside up again. Luigi is flung into the sky!

**What will happen to Luigi now?
It's up to you to make the decisions that will
get him through the ups and downs of
this adventure!**

Nintendo® Adventure Books Available in Mammoth:

**DOUBLE TROUBLE
LEAPING LIZARDS
MONSTER MIX-UP
KOOPA CAPERS
PIPE DOWN!
DOORS TO DOOM
DINOSAUR DILEMMA
FLOWN THE KOOPA**

LEAPING LIZARDS
By Clyde Bosco

MAMMOTH

*To Juana and Kelly
who inspired us to play with power*

This book is a work of fiction. Names, characters,
places and incidents are either the product of the
author's imagination or are used fictitiously. Any
resemblance to actual events or locales or persons,
living or dead, is entirely coincidental.

First published in the USA 1991 by Pocket Books,
a division of Simon & Schuster
First published in Great Britain 1992 by Mammoth
an imprint of Reed Consumer Books Ltd
Michelin House, 81 Fulham Road, London SW3 6RB
and Auckland, Melbourne, Singapore and Toronto

Reprinted 1991 (four times), 1992 (four times), 1993 (three times)

Copyright © 1991 by Nintendo. All Rights Reserved.
Cover artwork copyright © 1991 Nintendo

Nintendo, Super Mario Bros. and Mario, Luigi, Princess Toadstool,
Mushroom King, Cobrat and Toad are trademarks of Nintendo.

ISBN 0 7497 1001 2

A CIP catalogue record for this title
is available from the British Library

Printed in Great Britain
by Cox & Wyman Ltd, Reading, Berkshire

This paperback is sold subject to the condition
that it shall not, by way of trade or otherwise,
be lent, resold, hired out, or otherwise circulated
without the publisher's prior consent in any form
of binding or cover other than that in which
it is published and without a similar condition
including this condition being imposed
on the subsequent purchaser.

Creative Media Applications, Inc.
Series developed by Dan Oehlsen, Lary Rosenblatt &
Barbara Stewart
Art direction by Fabia Wargin Design
Cover painting by Greg Wray
Puzzle art by Josie Koehne
Edited by Eloise Flood
Special thanks to Ruth Ashby, Lisa Clancy, Paolo Pepe &
George Sinfield

Dear Game Player:

You are about to guide me through a great adventure. As you read this book, you will help me decide where to go and what to do. Whether I succeed or fail is up to you.

At the end of every chapter, you will make choices that determine what happens next. Special puzzles will help you decide what I should do—if you can solve them. The chapters in this book are in a special order. Sometimes you must go backward in order to go forward, if you know what I mean.

Along the way, you'll find many different items to help me with my quest. When you read that I have found something, such as an anchor, you'll see a box like the one below:

> *** Luigi now has the anchor. ***
> Turn to page 91.

Use page 121 to keep track of the things you collect and to keep score.

Good luck!
Driplessly yours,

Luigi

"Look out below!" Luigi yells. He dives headfirst into the Central Pipe that sticks up from the floor of the Mario Bros. plumbing workshop. Tumbling through steamy darkness, he passes dripping faucets, hissing valves and the glowing red eyes of wayward alligators. In minutes, he plunges from the Brooklyn plumbing shop to the Mushroom Kingdom, deep below the surface of the Earth.

Thump! Luigi drops out of the lower end of the great metal pipe and lands in a mound of spongy pink mushrooms.

"Two minutes fifty-eight seconds," he says, inspecting the dial on his plumber's stopwatch. "Not a bad time at all."

Unlike most of his journeys to the Mushroom Kingdom, this time there's no hurry. Usually Luigi and and his older brother, Mario, race down to the mysterious world to rescue Princess Toadstool, or to save the palace, or to perform some other heroic task. But today's visit is strictly for fun.

"Spread the blankets and start roasting those weenies," the tall, skinny plumber sings. "It's almost time for lunch."

Luigi slicks back his black mustache, straightens the straps of his bright green overalls, and hops onto the brick sidewalk that zig-zags through the Mushroom Kingdom. He bounces along the road, past small stone pyramids and wooden staircases that lead nowhere. Above his head, brick ledges and metal cubes hang in the air, suspended by some mysterious force.

"Ah," Luigi chirps. "It's a beautiful day for a picnic." He removes his green cap and lets the sun warm the top of his head.

Just then, two Goomba fungus monsters dart out from a clump of shrubs and charge toward Luigi's feet.

"Pests!" says Luigi. He jumps lightly, landing on the small brown creatures' flat heads. They scurry back to the bushes.

The plumber pauses by a heap of old, rusty pipes. "I stashed some equipment in these pipes last time I was here," he says. "You never know when you might need supplies. Now where did I leave those wings the princess gave me? Was it down that pipe to the left? Or was it just ahead, on the right?"

Solve this puzzle to find out which piece of emergency equipment Luigi finds in the Mushroom Kingdom:

- Follow the trail through the pipes. Along the way, you'll pass several junctions. Choose any branch you want and record the number of wrenches on that branch. Follow the pipes until you reach the exit. Then add up the total number of wrenches you collected on your trip and read the instructions at the bottom of the page. They'll tell you which item Luigi picks up.

If you pass a total of seven wrenches, Luigi has the anchor.

If you pass a total of five or six wrenches, Luigi has the frog suit.

If you pass a total of four wrenches, Luigi has the wings.

Turn to page 5.

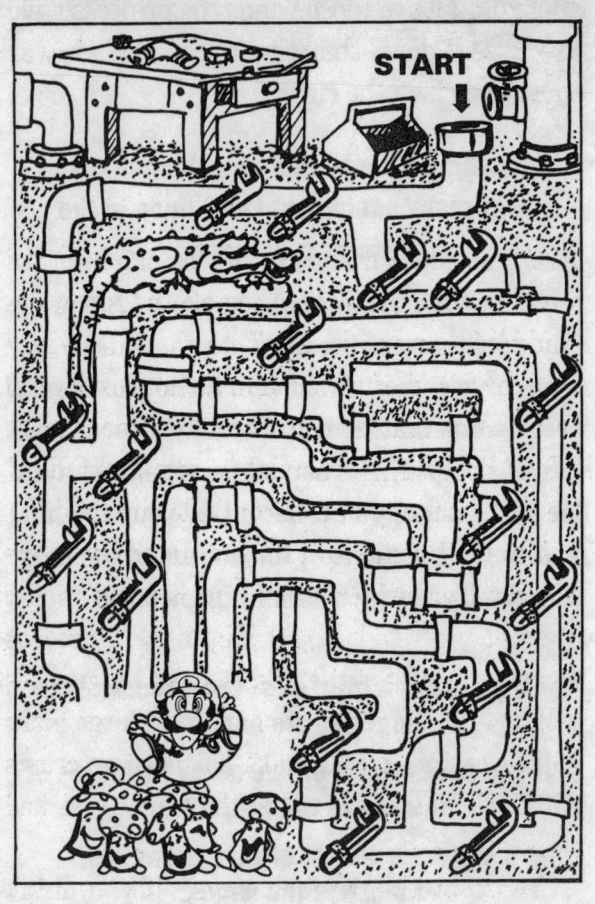

Luigi spots his friends at the top of a hill. "Hi guys!" he calls, and bounces off the sidewalk. "Did I miss any of the eats?"

As he marches up the hill, he notices several shiny coins scattered in the blue-green moss. "Hey," he says, "this must be my lucky day." He pockets the coins and continues up the hill.

Mario, Luigi's older and slightly more famous brother, is sitting on a plaid picnic blanket with Her Royal Highness, Princess Toadstool. Most of the food is gone. Luigi gazes longingly at the remains of an extra-large pizza with everything. All that's left is some crusts and a pile of anchovies that the princess picked off her slices.

"Little brother," Mario says, "if you didn't sleep till noon every day, you wouldn't have this problem." He smacks his lips and swallows the final bite of his toasted cheese sandwich.

"Good afternoon, Luigi," says the princess.

She sips delicately from a cone-shaped teacup. "Mario was just telling me about the time he saved the entire city of Topeka, Kansas from a flood."

Luigi is about to explain that it was he, not his older brother, who unclogged the giant overflowing bathtub at the last moment, siphoning away the terrible wall of water. Suddenly, a loud, high-pitched squeal fills the air. A two-foot-tall mushroom wearing a red polka dot turban runs up the hill.

"It's Toad," Mario says, jumping up from the blanket. "And I don't think he's here for the picnic!"

*** Luigi collects 5 coins. ***
Turn to page 64.

In the distance, Luigi sees Morton, paddling away desperately.

"You caused all this trouble, Morton," Luigi shouts. "Now you're going to fix it."

He swims furiously after Morton. As the turtle tries to crawl onto an island, Luigi launches himself out of the water and tackles Morton. He grabs the turtle by his shell and flips him over onto his back.

"Rrrrr!" Morton growls, flailing his tiny arms furiously. But no matter how he struggles, he's unable to right himself.

"Start talking, turtle," says Luigi. "Or I'll leave you for the Cheep Cheeps."

Morton roars and flails his scaly arms and legs until he's completely exhausted. "All right, plumber," he grumbles at last. "It's like this. . . ."

Turn to page 79.

4

"Watch," says Luigi. He races down the corridor toward Iggy. "This'll be like taking candy from a baby."

Iggy stands still as the plumber closes in. Then, just as Luigi is about to grab the whistle, the turtle ducks and pulls his head into his bumpy green shell.

Wha-bang! Luigi sails over Iggy and slams into a metal fuse box. He slumps to the floor, a look of surprise on his face.

Iggy pops back out of his shell. "Hoo, hoo!" he cackles. "I learned that trick from you plumbers."

The turtle trudges up to Mario, who backs away slightly, ready to jump at the first wrong move from the turtle. Instead, Iggy merely hands him a piece of paper. "Read it before you do anything stupid," he warns.

Mario takes out a pair of reading glasses and examines the yellowed page. He reads the paper aloud. "In compliance with Fungus Law X-27B, a Magic Silver Whistle may be sounded only by its rightful owner. Anyone else using the whistle is in violation of the Mushroom Kingdom Legal Code. This offense is punishable by up to seven years in the Sponge Mines."

"Hey, how did you get to be the rightful owner?" asks Luigi as he regains his feet and stumbles toward the group.

"Read on," says Iggy, sneering.

"The aforementioned Magic Silver Whistle shall become the rightful possession of whoever wins the International Mushroom Games," Mario continues. "Said games are to be held in a neutral area of the Mushroom Kingdom, every six years."

The princess takes the document from Mario's hands and studies it carefully. "It looks legal," she concludes.

Mario and Luigi stare at each other. "Six years!" they wail at the same time.

Iggy rocks back and forth in glee.

"Wait a minute!" says the princess. She snaps open the large gold-and-emerald locket that hangs from her neck. Removing a small notebook, she thumbs through it. "According to my date book, the next Mushroom Games are in three weeks!" she announces.

"So soon?" Iggy asks, surprised. "I thought I cheated, um, won that contest more recently than that." He rubs his lumpy green chin. "Well, I'd better start training."

Iggy shuffles off down the corridor, his toenails clicking on the paneled metal.

Solve this puzzle to see what happens next:

• Find a correct path from the four heroes to Iggy Koopa. Start on any one of the tiles closest to the heroes. Move up, down, left, or right until you reach Iggy. You may not move diagonally, and you may not cross the same tile pattern more than twice. If you can trace a path this way, then the heroes should follow Iggy. If you think it can't be done, then the four heroes should leave.

If you think the heroes should follow Iggy and try to grab the whistle, turn to page 44.

If you think the heroes should go back to their flying carpet and leave, turn to page 97.

"Going down," Luigi mutters. He tumbles through the air.

Fortunately, he's high above Water Land, instead of the Koopahari Desert or Pipe Land. A few hundred feet below, water stretches out in every direction.

"Bombs away!" Luigi shouts, curling himself into a cannonball.

He can see a cluster of Cheep Cheeps below him. They flap wildly, trying to get out of his way. Then the plummeting plumber plunges into the water.

> If Luigi has the anchor, turn to page 50.
> If Luigi doesn't have the anchor,
> turn to page 7.

"... The Mushroom Kingdom Royals!" Feldspar shouts. "They're the new champs!"

"Yay!" Toad cheers. He jumps up and down with glee, stomping on the princess's delicate toes.

"Hooray!" shouts Princess Toadstool. She's so excited about winning that she doesn't even notice the pain in her foot.

Feldspar presents the team with a Hoopster-shaped trophy and also gives them fifty coins. Mario and Luigi bow to each other, and do the secret plumbers' handshake. Mario even gives the king a big hug.

"Ah-ah-*achoo!*" he sneezes happily.

Just then Luigi notices Iggy Koopa, slinking away from the field. "Slow down, Iggy!" he yells. The six champions scramble over to the sneaky turtle.

"Cough up that whistle!" Luigi commands.

Iggy unfastens the silver chain and dangles

the small whistle above Luigi's anxious palm. "You can have it," he snarls. "But you've got to pay me five coins first."

"What?" shout Mario and the princess.

"Listen, shellbrain," says Luigi angrily. "If you think we're gonna—"

Iggy reaches into his pocket and takes out another brown, tattered piece of paper. "In accordance with Fungus Law W-16-N7..."

"Okay, okay!" grumbles Luigi, admitting defeat. He hands Iggy five of the shiny coins he picked up during his travels through the Mushroom Kingdom. The turtle pockets the coins, hands Luigi the whistle, and walks away in search of someone new to pick on.

"Well?" cries the princess, shaking Luigi's shoulder. "What're you waiting for?"

Luigi puts the whistle to his lips and blows. It makes no sound. The whistle turns bright green for a moment, then disappears completely. With a thunderclap and a flash of blue light, the eight-foot white rabbit changes into a six-foot, purple-robed king.

*** Luigi collects 45 coins. ***
Turn to page 54.

"The second event will be the Beetlebowl!" shouts Feldspar.

Once again, the crowd cheers. A brass band plays the Mushroom Kingdom national anthem. Then Bowser Koopa, ruler of the turtles and the worst villain in all the Mushroom Kingom, pushes his way up to the band. He forces them to play the Grand Koopa March. By the time the frightened musicians have finished verse twelve of "How Green Was My Belly," the stadium has been set up for the next event.

The center of the great field has been roped off to form a diamond. In the middle of the diamond sits a cluster of basketball-shaped Hoopster beetles. In each corner of the field stands a large, empty bucket.

"All members of each team will compete in this event," Feldspar explains. He raises an orange Hoopster bug above his head. "There will be four beetles on the field at all times.

Each team must try to drop one beetle into any of their opponents' buckets. At the same time, you must stop your opponents from sinking one into your bucket. Any questions?"

"Yes!" shouts everyone in the stadium.

"Too bad," replies the penguin. "Organize your teams now."

Luigi twirls his black mustache, trying to decide which of the Royals should try to dunk the beetles and which should play defense. "Okay," he says, after a while. "Here's the plan...."

Solve this puzzle to help decide what the Royals should do:

• These athletes are all competing in the Mushroom Games. Can you find them in this word search?

COBRAT ROCKY MARIO LEMMY
IGGY ANGUS LUIGI SPIKE
FIRESNAKES WENDY ROY WOOSTER
TOAD THE KING

• Words go up, down, across and backwards. The leftover letters will help you decide how to organize the Beetleball team.

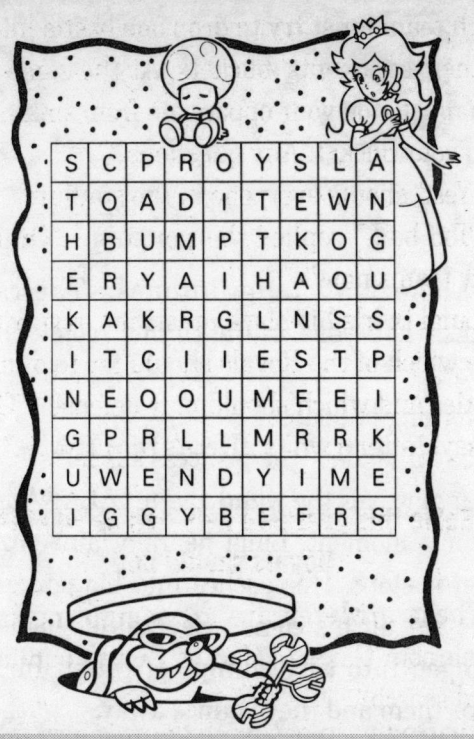

If you think Mario, Luigi and the princess should dunk and the rest of the team should defend, turn to page 39.

If you think the king, the princess, Wooster and Toad should dunk and the rest should defend, turn to page 102.

If you think Luigi and the princess should dunk and the rest of the team should defend, turn to page 85.

"Alakazam!" Luigi intones. The rabbit blinks. Everyone in the throne room watches intently.

Nothing happens.

"Say it louder," the princess suggests.

Luigi waves the wand again. "ALAKAZAM!"

For a moment, Luigi hears a faint buzzing. Then it stops. He reaches into his pocket and pulls out all his coins. Several of them have changed into tiny clumps of rabbit fur. He drops them and they bounce away.

"Try a different magic word," Mario offers.

"Yeah," says Toad. "Try Alakazam."

"He just tried that," the princess snaps.

"Oh," says Toad. "Then try Alakazook!"

Once more, Luigi flourishes the wand at the king. "And awa-a-a-a-y we go!"

*** Luigi loses 5 coins. ***
Turn to page 104.

9

Over the next three weeks, Luigi, Mario, Toad and the princess train for the International Mushroom Games. Luigi practices the long jump, leaping over almost everything in the Mushroom Kingdom. Mario works out by picking up empty turtle shells and hurling them as far as he can.

The princess hones her surfing skills. She also swims up several waterfalls, and climbs to the top of Mount Morel, the tallest mountain in the Mushroom Kingdom.

Toad works out a little. But he spends most of his time helping Wooster keep an eye on the king—which is a workout in itself. Eight-foot-tall rabbits are not easily entertained. His Highness has been nibbling on curtains, bedposts, sculptures and picture frames. In fact, everything in the palace shows signs of wear from the rabbit's teeth.

"We've just got to win!" sobs Wooster, as the

day of the games draws near. "If we don't, the palace will be ruined!"

Luigi and his friends will have a tough time winning. Solve this puzzle to find out why.

• Queen Trufflessa IV was the greatest athlete in Mushroom Kingdom history. This is what she said after she set the record for the 26-mile-long hot dog eating contest:

"WINNER, SCHMINNER! HURRY UP,
I WANT MY DINNER!"

• Look for the words of that famous quotation in this grid. Cross them out as you find them. The leftover words tell you why it will be hard for our heroes to win the games.

WANT	EVERY	WINNER
UP	DINNER	BODY
ELSE	MY	HURRY
SCHMINNER	CHEATS	I

Turn to page 30.

"Up, up, and away!" shouts Luigi. He dashes up to the high bar and hurls himself into the air. With the help of his magic equipment, he clears the bar easily and dives into the great green pipe.

"Two down, one to go," he says when he drops out of the other end of the pipe. "This is the one that counts."

With all his might, Luigi flings his tall, skinny body across the playing field. He lands at the 152-Mushroom-Meter mark, just two units further than Cobrat.

Then Iggy Koopa comes sailing out of the giant pipe. The turtle is not quite as good a jumper as Luigi. He leaps into the air and drops towards the 140-Mushroom-Meter mark.

"I win!" Luigi thinks.

But just before he hits the ground, Iggy takes out a large spray can. "Watch this," he cackles. He pushes the trigger on the can and it fires off a blast of smelly green steam. Iggy shoots back into the air. He lands with a thud next to a marker that says "160 MUSHROOM METERS."

"First place . . . Iggy Koopa!" calls Feldspar. "Second place . . . Luigi." He hands a wooden medal to the plumber.

Nervously, Luigi heads back to the bench to total up the medals and find out who wins.

*** **The Royals get one wooden medal.** ***
Turn to page 57.

"... You're our man, Mario," says Luigi, and tips his cap to his older brother.

"If you say so," Mario replies. He gets up from the bench and takes his place with the others at the north end of the field.

The referee waddles up to the starting line. He waves a small green flag high over his head. "On your mark. Get set. GO!" he shouts as he brings the flag down.

The four competitors leap into action. Grunting and panting, they climb the brick ledges and boxes that begin the course. Rocky Wrench takes an early lead, diving from one platform to another, but the others are only a few yards behind.

Hand over hand, Mario moves along the course, in last place by a few paces. He hangs from a shiny metal box for a moment and inspects it. The top of the cube pops open and a small, glowing mushroom falls out.

"A Super Mushroom!" he cries excitedly. "Now we're getting somewhere."

When he grabs the magical fungus, he's suddenly charged with energy. He swings onto the top of the box and examines the ledge above his head. "Going up," he calls, and smashes a hole in the ledge with his fist. Then he jumps through the hole and races along the top of the ledge. He thumps his chest. "Ah, I feel so fit!"

When Mario reaches the next brick ledge, he jumps up and smashes a hole in it, too. Unfortunately, Angus Boomer is standing right above him at the time. The 600-pound turtle falls through—and lands on the plumber.

"*Aaaggh!*" Mario cries despairingly.

Crash, crash, crash! Angus and Mario tumble over the side of the ledge and fall through three flimsy wooden platforms before splashing into the edge of the pool.

"Out of my way!" Angus shouts. He bats Mario aside with a giant paw and swims away.

It takes Mario a few seconds to come to his senses. The Super Mushroom has worn off. Shaking his head, he plunges forward. The plumber navigates the waterway with expert skill. But he's now far behind the others. By the time he reaches the vines and starts climbing, Rocky Wrench has already crossed the finish line.

Meanwhile, Roy and Angus are boarding their magic carpets.

"Allow me," snarls the Koopa brat as he yanks the rug out from under Angus. The huge turtle plummets into the patch of snapping, snarling Muncher plants. "Tsk, tsk," Roy says, and sails across the finish line.

A few minutes later, Mario floats to the end of the course. Exhausted, he trudges back to the bench.

"Third place!" shouts Feldspar. He hands Mario a medal made of pure chocolate.

*** **The Royals get one chocolate medal.** ***
Turn to page 15.

"I'll meet you there!" calls Luigi. He dashes off to the palace. "Mario might be more famous, and maybe even a bit smarter," he pants. "But nobody's *faster* than me!"

He races along, hopping over snapping turtles and Goombas that get in his way. There's no time to bonk them properly.

Soon he reaches the white marble walls of the palace. He bounces past the royal doormen, asleep at their posts, and charges down the hall into the throne room.

"Uh-oh," Luigi says as he crashes through the massive wooden double doors.

The palace is usually spotless, thanks to the attention of Wooster, the chief mushroom assistant. If Wooster had his way, no one would enter the throne room until he passed a special no-smudge test.

But there's no sign of Wooster. Even more troubling, there's no sign of the king. Instead,

Morton Koopa, a large, armored turtle, is lumbering around the chamber. As Luigi watches in alarm, Morton dips a paw into a jar he's carrying and smears a fistful of peanut butter on the royal walls.

"Rarrr!" Morton growls. "I haven't had so much fun in weeks!" In one hand, he holds a ruby-tipped wand. He scrapes it against the royal blackboard. Luigi claps his hands over his ears to block out the horrible sound.

"Yikes!" Morton blurts, as he notices Luigi. "Time to go!" He darts toward an open window. Luigi lunges at the evil turtle.

Solve this puzzle to see what happens:

- Follow the trail from Luigi to Morton. Whenever you reach a blob of peanut butter, choose which way to go. When you land on either Morton or a window, follow the directions below.

**If you land on Morton Koopa, turn to page 98.
If you land on a window, turn to page 78.**

At last, the day of the games arrives.

"Welcome! Welcome!" squawks the official Mushroom Games referee, a penguin named Feldspar. He waddles back and forth proudly on a patch of blue grass in the center of the stadium, waving his flippers to get the crowd's attention.

Nearly every citizen of the Mushroom Kingdom has turned out for the great festival. Shoulder to shoulder, mushroom cap to mushroom cap, leaf to leaf, they pack the stands that have been set up in an open field near the palace. Thousands of assorted Goombas, Shyguys, Thwomps, and even Cheep Cheeps have traveled from the Koopahari Desert, Ice Land and beyond to enjoy the spectacle.

Hordes of Koopa Troopas and other foul-smelling monsters have been given special admittance to the Mushroom Kingdom so they can root for the Koopas and the other teams that will be competing.

Sitting on long wooden benches next to the field are the four teams who have signed up to play in the games. Six of the Koopa kids, including Morton and Iggy, form one team. Three pairs of huge, leering, twin turtles form another team—the Hammers. As Luigi and the princess argue over the name of their team, another awful group marches by. It includes a red serpent named Cobrat, a pair of blazing four-foot-long Firesnakes, a vicious armadillo named Spike, and two Bloober Nannies.

"Introducing . . . the Snakes!" Feldspar announces. Spike taps him on the shoulder and whispers in his ear. "Excuse me . . . the Sneaks!" the penguin says.

"I've got it!" says the princess. "Since we're representing the Mushroom Kingdom, and some of us are royal"—she looks at the king sadly—"let's call ourselves the Mushroom Kingdom Royals."

Mario makes a face, but he holds his tongue in deference to her royal highness. "Well," says Luigi. "Since you got to name the team, I get to be team captain." There's no time to argue, as the penguin referee starts talking once more.

"In each event, athletes will have a chance to

win a medal," Feldspar explains. "Tin medals are for first place. Wooden medals are for second place. Chocolate medals are for third place. Anyone who eats his or her medal shall be disqualified."

Mario, Luigi, Princess Toadstool and Toad listen to the rules carefully. Wooster struggles to keep the king from hopping away.

"The team that wins the most medals will be the new Mushroom Games Champions," Feldspar continues. He straightens his bow tie. "Let the games begin!"

As you read the next few chapters, use a separate piece of paper to keep track of the medals the Mushroom Kingdom Royals win.

Turn to page 111.

14

Luigi walks down the tunnel. The walls are covered with a tangle of wires, levers, control panels and circuit boxes. Small glass portholes on both sides of the corridor display the outside ocean. Schools of electric jellyfish drift by, but they pay no attention to him.

He turns right at the first corner and runs smack into Mario, Toad, and the princess.

"What are you doing here?" Luigi asks, startled.

"We've been following you on my flying carpet," answers Princess Toadstool.

"Wooster was looking for carrot recipes in the royal library, so he could make the king something for dinner," Toad explains. "He came across a book about giant rabbits. According to the book, if we want to change the king back to normal, all we need is a magic silver whistle."

"The princess went to the Koopermarket to buy some snails yesterday," Mario adds. "And she remembers seeing a silver whistle around Iggy Koopa's neck."

"Jewelry is my specialty," the princess says modestly.

Mario walks over to his brother and places one hand on Luigi's shoulder. "We saw you heading towards Iggy's lab. We thought you might want a little help."

Luigi is very hurt. "I knew you'd never let me be a hero by myself," he grumbles.

"Cheer up, little brother," says Mario. "No one's going to get in your way. Besides, we had to tell you about the magic whistle."

"What about my whistle?" says a shrill voice.

All four adventurers turn at once. A few yards away stands a five-foot-tall turtle wearing glasses. The wind from an air duct above his head tosses his purple hair wildly.

"Iggy Koopa!" they exclaim in unison. Around his neck, for all to see, is a small whistle on a shiny silver chain.

Turn to page 8.

15

"Oh, all right," says Luigi. He throws up his hands. "Let Wooster be team captain."

"Wait a minute!" Mario protests. "What about me and the princess?"

"Please-oh-please-oh-please," Wooster pleads. "Let me do it!"

"Oh, fine," says the princess.

"Goody!" Wooster smiles and stands up in front of the group. After beaming for a few seconds, he looks concerned. "Er—what is it that I'm supposed to do?" he asks.

"Choose who jumps!" everyone shouts at him angrily.

"Oh," Wooster says. "That's easy." He skips around the bench, looking at his teammates closely. "I think it should be . . . the king."

"Brilliant!" declares Mario.

Beaming, Wooster leads the rabbit to the jumping track and gives him a gentle shove. "Hey! No fair!" shouts Iggy, from the Koopas' bench.

With one tremendous leap, the king bounds over the high bar, sails through the pipe, and lands at the end of the field, more than 600 Mushroom Meters away.

"First place!" shouts Feldspar. "And you get two tin medals, your Majesty. One for winning the contest, and one for setting a new Mushroom Kingdom record!"

> *** The Royals get two tin medals. ***
> Turn to page 57.

16

"Can't I leave this palace for five minutes without everything falling apart?" the princess grumbles. She straightens the chain of her gold and emerald necklace and looks angrily around the throne room for more signs of destruction.

"Um—your Majesty . . ." Wooster squeaks. He holds his hands behind his back, shifting his feet nervously.

"I'm not through complaining yet!" snaps the princess. She paces back and forth, getting angrier and angrier. "Where's my surfboard? My jewlery box is on the floor! The strings are missing from my tennis racquet! Hey—wait a minute!" She stops and looks at the empty throne. "Where's my father?"

"That's what I wanted to mention to you, your Highness," mumbles Wooster. The chief mushroom assistant takes one hand from behind his back. Sadly, he holds up a small, fluffy, white rabbit.

The animal is kicking, but Wooster grips him tightly. Luigi notes that the rabbit has a thin black mustache and a tiny, onion-shaped crown. The rabbit looks confused.

"It's the king!" Luigi gasps.

"I was in the garage, trying to untangle the royal air hoses," moans Wooster. "While I was gone, that horrible turtle zapped the king with a magic wand."

"Achoo!" Mario sneezes. "I'm allergic to rabbit fur."

"That's just great," says the princess. "We need that wand, and fast!"

"Relax, princess," says Luigi. "There's no need to get nervous. I'm at your service."

**If Luigi has the wand, turn to page 69.
If Luigi doesn't have the wand,
turn to page 110.**

17

"Cha-a-a-arge!" shout the princess and the two plumbers. Waving their arms madly, they race to the center of the field.

For a few minutes the center of the diamond is a blur of fur, scales, mushrooms and plumbers. Some of the monsters are pounding each other with their fists. Most are simply scrambling to catch the slippery beetles.

"Got one!" shouts Lemmy Koopa, clutching one of the Hoopsters.

Spike the armadillo grabs the beetle from the rainbow-haired reptile. "Let's trade," he cackles, handing Lemmy a rotten melon. Spike lights a fuse on the end of the melon. It blows up, splattering Lemmy with smelly goo.

Meanwhile, Toad, Wooster and the rabbit king guard their bucket. But after eating all the grass in their goal area, the king hops off in search of new things to nibble.

"Come back!" shouts Wooster, following him.

"Uh-oh," mutters Toad.

Wendy O. Koopa runs up to the Royals' bucket, steps right over Toad and slams the beetle into the goal. Then Cobrat slithers over, with a Hoopster gripped in his fangs.

Toad holds both arms in front of him in an effort to push back the giant red snake, but Cobrat slips between his legs, rears up, and drops the beetle into the bucket.

Next the Sledge Brothers, the biggest turtles Toad has ever seen, stomp toward the goal.

The royal mushroom retainer doesn't even try to stop them. "Yipe!" Toad squeals. He scurries out of the way, barely dodging the mammoth turtles' powerful feet.

Mario, Luigi and the princess have a Hoopster, and are passing it back and forth as they work toward the nearest bucket. But before they get a chance to dunk, the game is over!

"Third place, event over," yells Feldspar as one of the Sledge Brothers deposits his beetle.

***The Royals do not get a medal for this event. ***

Turn to page 47.

18

Luigi grips the rail with one hand and his cap with the other. He closes his eyes and braces himself for the ship to crash.

Seconds pass, but nothing happens. Finally, Luigi opens his eyes. To his amazement, the ship has stopped its descent a few inches above the water. It drifts into the mouth of a huge metal pipe sticking out of the sea.

The Doom Ship sinks down the pipe. It drops for about two hundred feet. Then it gently touches down in a large, square room.

"Where are we?" Luigi mutters, gazing about him. Wires, light bulbs, meters and control panels are everywhere.

"This must one of Iggy's secret labs," Luigi thinks. But when he looks toward the steering wheel, the turtle is gone.

Quickly, the plumber jumps to the floor. There's no sign of Iggy. "What now?" Luigi mutters. Finally, he heads toward one of several tunnels that lead out of the room. Before he reaches the tunnel entrance, he stumbles over a metal hatch in the floor.

"Hmmm," says Luigi. "Should I check out the tunnel, or should I look below?"

Solve this puzzle for a clue:

• Read the chart on the right, and connect all the pairs of numbers on the list in the drawing below. Then read the message that appears. It'll help you decide what Luigi should do next.

• Connect the following numbers:

12-18	6-12	32-33	9-10	15-21	27-28
8-14	15-16	20-21	17-18	13-19	26-27
10-11	19-25	31-32	33-34	5-11	13-14
25-31	28-34	8-9	20-26	16-17	

```
 1   2   3   4   5   6
 T   R   A   T   S
 7   8   9  10  11  12
     A   D   I   U   Q
13  14  15  16  17  18
 B       S   A       M   E
19  20  21  22  23  24
     E   A   T   P   E
25  26  27  28  29  30
 L   O   W       E   Z
31  32  33  34  35  36
```

If you think Luigi should climb down the hatch, turn to page 52.

If you think Luigi should head into the tunnel, turn to page 33.

43

19

"I wonder how Iggy won the Mushroom Games in the first place," Luigi ponders. "Do you think he cheated?"

"Does Fort Koopa need sweeping?" quips Mario. "He cheated. Let's get him!"

The four friends tiptoe after Iggy. Mario and Luigi move ahead. But just as they're about to grab him, Iggy whirls and reaches for a lever on the wall. He pulls it down.

Whoosh! A blast of water gushes down from a pipe in the ceiling. The heroes are washed backward down the hall. They tumble head over heels, and finally land on the floor in a soggy heap.

Soaking wet and disappointed, the four heroes head back to the flying carpet.

> *** If Luigi had the wings, they have been washed away. ***
>
> Turn to page 97.

20

Toad, the princess, and the two plumbers gather as many picnic supplies as they can and hurry to the palace. Snapping turtles and Goomba mushrooms scurry out of their way as the group marches along the crooked brick road. They climb the grand staircase to the large, white marble castle.

As they enter the main hall, Princess Toadstool spies the two royal doormen, Gerkins and Brock. Both are asleep at their posts. She doesn't say anything to them, but she looks angry. And when she pushes open the great double doors to the throne room, the princess's face turns beet red.

The king is nowhere to be found. Neither is Wooster, the chief mushroom assistant. Neither is Morton Koopa. There's nothing in the throne room but a colossal mess.

Peanut butter covers every inch of the royal woodwork. Everywhere, Princess Toadstool sees broken fragments of her china cups and saucers. Jagged turtle toothmarks mar several pieces of the king's prized melon collection. At last, she explodes with rage.

"This is too much!" she cries. She peers out the window, but there's no sign of Morton Koopa. Then she looks behind the throne and finds Wooster crouching there, shaking with fear.

"H-hello, your Highness," whimpers the tall, pale mushroom. "How was your picnic?"

Turn to page 37.

21

The next few contests go badly for the Mushroom Kingdom Royals. Wooster comes in last in the Turnip Toss. While everyone else throws their vegetables for distance and accuracy, the chief mushroom assistant arranges his in neat piles on the ground.

"They look so much better this way," Wooster argues, appealing to Feldspar. But the referee only scowls, and the Royals get no medal for the event.

Princess Toadstool loses the Waterfall Race, also. Iggy Koopa spins her around so she ends up pointing the wrong way. Instead of swimming up the waterfall, she heads deep into the pool at the bottom. And before she realizes her mistake, the race is over.

The only bright moment comes when Toad enters the Fungus Lift. Everyone, including the Mario Brothers, is astounded when the mushroom retainer lifts twelve thousand pounds. Not even the Sledge Brothers can do that. The Royals get a tin medal.

As the sun begins to set, the Mushroom Games are almost over. Only one event is left—the Super Triple Jump.

Solve this puzzle for a look ahead:

• The plumbers, the princess and Toad are about to practice for the final event. The chart at the top shows how high each can jump. Follow the arrow next to each athlete and cross out every hurdle which is too high for him or her to clear. The letters under the remaining hurdles spell out something extra the plumbers will get if they win the games.

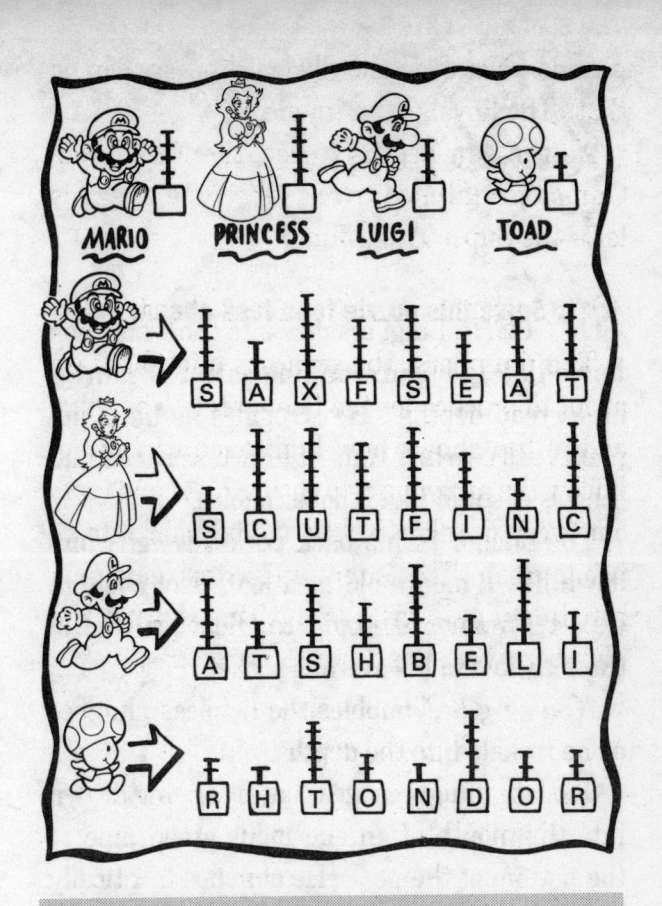

	MARIO	PRINCESS	LUIGI	TOAD
MARIO	S A	X F	S E	A T
PRINCESS	S C	U T	F I	N C
LUIGI	A T	S H	B E	L I
TOAD	R H	T O	N D	O R

The Royals get one tin medal.
Turn to page 55.

49

22

SPLOOSH! Luigi crashes into the water and immediately begins sinking into the murky, blue-green depths. He struggles as he plummets past swirling tufts of brown seaweed and schools of squid-like Bloober babies.

The anchor in his back pocket weighs him down like a month-old meatloaf. Not even an expert swimmer like Luigi can float with one of those tucked in his overalls pocket.

"*G-a-r-r-g-l-e,*" bubbles the helpless plumber as he rockets into the depths.

Too late, Luigi realizes that he's being drawn into the mouth of an enormous green pipe at the bottom of the pool. He clutches frantically at seaweed strands, lotus leaves, and anything else within his reach. But nothing prevents him from spiralling into the churning whirpool.

"*A-a-a-r-g-h!*" he gurgles. Then he's siphoned into the dark mouth of the giant pipe. Everything goes black.

A few hours later, Luigi is awakened by a sharp pain in his back.

"Ooooh," he groans, and pulls the anchor from the back pocket of his soggy overalls. "Where's my cap?"

Luigi gazes about his new surroundings. "Wait a minute . . . where am I?" he asks.

Above his head are thirty different pipe openings. On all sides are clusters of multi-colored pipes. Great networks of tubing stretch as far as the eye can see.

Luigi now knows where he is. "Oh no! I'm in Pipe Land!" he wails. "It could take me weeks to get out of here—and I didn't even have lunch!"

Luigi grits his teeth in frustration. Then he climbs to his feet and begins the long journey home. By the time he escapes from the maze of metal tubes, the Koopas will surely have completed their evil plans. Even worse, Mario might save the day without him! Either way, Luigi's plans are ruined.

GAME OVER!

23

Luigi decides to take a look below. He lifts the hatch open and climbs down a ladder into a steamy, dimly lit room.

Suddenly his foot slips on one of the slimy ladder rungs. Luigi falls off the ladder and drops into a huge pool filled with warm, salty water. He coughs, sputters—and freezes. Staring right at him are eight pairs of bloodshot, baseball-sized eyes.

"Bloobers!" Luigi thrashes frantically.

A school of giant, white, squid-like creatures slides up to the frightened plumber and surrounds him. He can't get away!

Solve this puzzle to find out what happens next:

- Start on the bubble in the center of the page. If Luigi has the frog suit, move one space up. If not, move either one space left or one space right. The arrow on each new space will show you where to go next. When you land on a Bloober or on Luigi, follow the directions below.

52

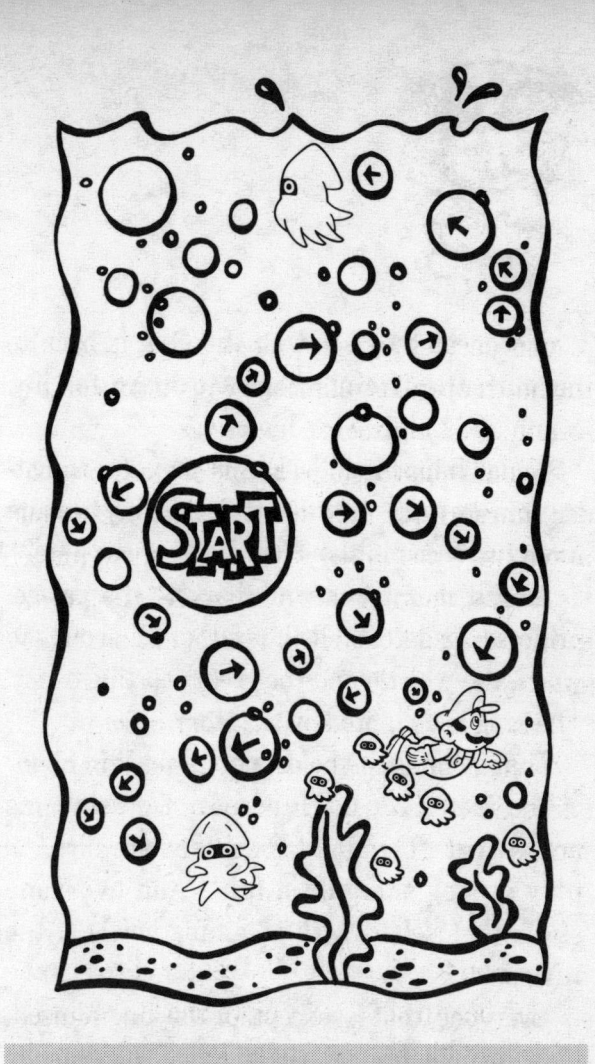

If you land on Luigi, turn to page 67.
If you land on a Bloober, turn to page 108.

24

As soon as they see that the king is back to normal, the friends begin to jump for joy. Mario and Luigi do the high five.

"What happened?" asks his majesty, adjusting his crown. "I was sitting in my throne room two seconds ago. How did I get out here?"

As the champions walk back to the palace, princess Toadstool tells her father all about the wand, the whistle and the great sporting event. The king is delighted by the story.

That evening, he holds a great feast in honor of the Mario Bros. Hundreds of mushrooms are invited. The finest musicians are hired to play during the gala affair. And everyone stuffs themselves with steaming bowls of the ravioli.

Everyone, that is, except for the king himself. He just smiles and nibbles on a nice, juicy carrot.

YOU WIN! — GAME OVER!

25

"Okay," Luigi tells his team. "I'm not sure which team is ahead in the standings, but it's close. This jump could decide it."

"We've just got to win," says the princess. "We won't get another chance to win that magic whistle for six years."

"Six years?" groans Wooster. He brushes away the king, who has been nibbling on his hat. "The palace will be ruined by then!"

"So wish me luck, guys," Luigi continues. "I'm doing the Super Triple Jump."

Mario scowls. "Why do you get to do it?"

"Because I'm captain," Luigi replies.

"Oh yeah?" snaps Princess Toadstool. "You've been running this show all day, and we haven't done that well. Why don't you let someone else make the decisions?"

"Let me be captain," says Wooster brightly.

"That's not what I had in mind," says the princess.

Meanwhile the crowd is becoming restless as it awaits the final event. In the center of the stadium, a high bar has been set up. Next to it, a huge pipe hangs by cables from a balloon above the field. A long area has been cleared for the third part of the jump.

"Ladies and gentlemen, monsters and mushrooms!" squawks Feldspar. "To compete in this event, you must clear the high bar, jump through the pipe, and then leap as far as you can. Whoever jumps farthest at the end will win the final tin medal. Are you ready?"

Iggy Koopa steps forward to jump for the Koopa team. Cobrat slithers up to jump for the Sneaks. None of the Hammers can jump very well—their legs are too short. They simply bow out of the competition.

"Good! The Hammers are out," says Luigi.

"Do I get to be team captain now?" Wooster asks.

> **If you think Wooster should be captain, and decide who jumps, turn to page 35.**
>
> **If you think Luigi should remain team captain, turn to page 89.**

26

"That's it, it's over," says Mario.

"Did we win?" asks Toad.

The princess snaps open her locket. She takes out a pencil and a notepad and begins to count up the medals that each team has won. But before she can finish, the penguin referee waddles to the center of the field.

The crowd falls silent.

"The judges have reached a decision!" Feldspar trumpets. "And the winner is..."

Here's how to add up the Royals's score: for each tin medal, score 10 points. For each wooden medal, score 5 points. For each chocolate medal, score 1 point. If the total is:

> 10 points or less, turn to page 72.
> 11 to 29 points, turn to page 66.
> 30 to 45 points, turn to page 13.
> 46 points or more, turn to page 72.

27

Luigi jumps onto the porch of the floating shack and knocks on the door.

"No one's home," a gruff, scratchy voice calls from within.

"Well, then," Luigi says cheerfully, "I'll let myself in and have a look around."

"Oh, no you won't!" shouts the same voice. The door swings open to reveal Morton Koopa. His three straggly hairs wave gracefully in the soft Water Land breeze.

Luigi jumps over the large turtle and looks about the cabin. He sees nothing but old socks and garbage. "You zapped the king with a magic wand," he accuses Morton. "What are you going to do about it?" He opens a box and wrinkles his nose at the awful smell that seeps out.

"Hey! Leave my stuff alone!" yells Morton as he tries to grab Luigi. But every time Morton lunges at Luigi, the plumber hops aside. Soon Morton—who's not known for his stamina—begins to tire. Finally, he waddles over to a box on one wall and flips open its lid. Then he presses a small red button.

"What does that do?" asks Luigi, standing still for a moment.

"You'll see," sneers Morton. He points with his scaly finger to one of the houseboat's dirty windows. There in the sky, a large black object approaches.

"The Doom Ship!" cries Luigi. "Just what I need." The Koopa family's floating battleship drifts over Morton's slimy boat. It looks like a cross between a pirate ship and a merry-go-round, festooned with propellers and steam pipes. On deck, Luigi glimpses Iggy Koopa, one of Morton's awful brothers. Just then, Morton bolts out the door.

"Come back here!" Luigi yells. He darts after the turtle.

From high above the houseboat, Iggy lowers a rope ladder to Morton. They shout something to each other in Koopanese. But when Iggy spots Luigi, he stops short and hauls the ladder back up again. The Doom Ship rises swiftly back into the sky. *"Arrrrgh,"* Morton growls. "Little brothers are so cowardly!" He dives into the water and swims frantically toward the next island.

"I resent that!" says Luigi. "And one of you has some explaining to do." He frowns as both reptiles start to escape. "But which brother should I go after?"

Solve this puzzle for a clue:

• There are two messages in this picture, but they've gotten mixed together. Swap all the odd-numbered letters in the two trails. When you're done, the trails will help you decide what Luigi should do next.

If you think Luigi should try to board the Doom Ship, turn to page 62.

If you think Luigi should go after Morton Koopa, turn to page 7.

28

With one terrific leap, Luigi jumps into the air and grabs one of the twisted metal bars that hang from the bottom of the Doom Ship. "I'd like to see Mario try that," he says to himself.

Carefully, he climbs up the side of the great ship, clinging to its warped wooden planks. Luigi is not especially afraid of heights, but he tries not to look down. In no time, he reaches the top.

He swings over the railing and onto the deck, and then dives behind a stack of crates marked "FRAGILE—PLEASE DROP." Iggy Koopa stands at the steering wheel of the ship, wearing a white backpack. The scrawny turtle doesn't seem to notice the plumber.

"Now's my chance," thinks Luigi. He crouches behind the crates, watching Iggy carefully. "I can scare the turtle off and take over the ship!"

Then he pauses, thinking hard. "Or should I wait here and see what happens?"

Solve this puzzle for help:

• Draw a straight line from each of the Doom Ship cannons in this drawing. Then cross out any of the letters in the boxes that your lines touch. The leftover letters spell out a secret message that will help you decide what Luigi should do next.

D	R	O	W	N
C	O	Z	E	P
O	U	T	A	M
H	W	P	P	O
O	R	V	L	E

If you think Luigi should confront Iggy Koopa, turn to page 100.

If you think Luigi should stay hidden, turn to page 114.

63

29

"It's terrible! It's horrible! It's . . . it's not good!" yelps Toad, the royal mushroom retainer, as he dashes up. "Morton Koopa's in the palace, and he's making a terrible mess."

"Ugh," Mario grunts. "Another Koopa attack. It seems like every time we stop one of those crummy turtles, another shows up."

"Thanks for coming to warn us, Toad," says the princess. She addresses the plumbers in her best mushroom royalty voice. "Let's hurry back to the palace. The king needs our help."

"I'll run ahead," Mario offers. "The king will want my protection right away."

"No!" Luigi shouts. "I can get there faster." When the princess looks the other way, he sticks his tongue out at his brother.

Mario grabs one of the cold, uneaten anchovies and plops it onto Luigi's tongue. Luigi spits it out indignantly.

"Let's all go together," Toad suggests.

"Hmm," says Princess Toadstool thoughtfully. "I just don't know what to do!"

Here's a clue to help you decide:

- Shade in all the spaces with an odd number of sides, and a secret message will be revealed.

If you think the four heroes should head to the palace together, turn to page 45.

If you think Luigi should run ahead and get there first, turn to page 27.

30

"... The Koopas!" announces Feldspar. "They're the Mushroom Games champions!"

Slowly, the crowds file out of the stadium. Our heroes stand in the field, pondering their defeat. It starts to drizzle.

"Nice try, guys," Iggy Koopa calls, sneering. He waddles up to the princess and places one greasy, green paw on her shoulder. "Tell you what," he says. "Because you tried so hard, I'll let you use my whistle anyway."

"Really?" The princess's eyes brighten.

"No," replies Iggy. "I was just kidding. Hee, hee!" He walks off.

"We'll get him next time," Luigi vows.

"Next time?" groans Wooster. "That's not for six years. By then, the King will have chewed up the entire Mushroom Kingdom!"

GAME OVER!

31

A great, slippery Bloober swishes up to Luigi. It waves one of its rubbery tentacles in front of the plumber's face and sprays him with a blast of bluish-black ink. Then it darts away to the other end of the tank.

"Yuck!" Luigi wipes the gooey syrup from his face. He swims after the Bloober. "I'll get you, you big rubber chicken!" he shouts. But suddenly, the corners of his vision become fuzzy. Looking back, he sees that he's swimming in a crazy, weaving pattern. His arms and legs seem to be moving in slow motion.

"That was a blast of Sleepy Ink, I think," Luigi says to himself. He yawns and paddles for a few more yards. Then he drifts into a deep sleep. He rolls over on his back in the water and floats away to dreamland.

When Luigi wakes, he's completely dry. He's lying flat on his back on the log bridge at the entrance to Water Land.

"How did I get here?" he says sleepily. "I was chasing Morton, and then I got on the Doom Ship, and then it landed in Iggy's lab, but I lost Iggy, and . . . I don't know!"

He sits up. "The one thing I do know is, I've got to find one of the Koopas and make them restore the king!"

Turn to page 7.

32

Luigi clicks the heels of his plumber boots together and waits until he has the attention of everyone in the room.

"Remain calm, everyone," he announces. "The younger, better-looking plumber is here. Everything is under control."

"What's that supposed to mean?" demands Mario. He's still sniffling because of the rabbit's fur.

Luigi twirls the ends of his glossy black mustache. "I've just had a little chat with Morton Koopa," he explains. "I convinced him to, uh, 'lend' me his magic wand. Whenever you're ready, I'll change the king back to his normal short-eared self."

"Take your time," Toad says, as he strokes the king's soft white fur. "I think he's kind of cute this way."

The furry monarch bites Toad's thumb.

"Ouch!" Toad shouts.

"Maybe you'd better get this over with," advises the princess.

"Have no fear my dear, your plumber is here with the magical gear!" Luigi sings as he bounces up to the throne.

The princess leans over to Mario. "Does he always act this way?" she whispers.

"Nah." Mario shakes his head. "He's usually a lot goofier."

Luigi pulls the ruby wand from a pocket in his overalls. "You know, I've never used one of these before," he says. "But it can't be much trickier than using a pipe wrench."

Wooster holds the royal rabbit at arms' length. "I hope this isn't going to be messy," he grumbles.

Luigi waves the wand in a circle. The rabbit king blinks. But nothing happens.

"Say a magic word," suggests the princess.

"Yeah, like Alakazook!" adds Toad.

"I think that's supposed to be Alakazam," Princess Toadstool says.

"I think it's supposed to be 'hurry up!'" says Mario impatiently.

"All right folks, here we go!" cries Luigi. He waves the ruby wand once more. This time, he shouts out a magic word.

Solve this puzzle for a clue:

Find a path from the fearless plumber to the rabbit king. The letters you cross along the way will spell out the correct magic word.

If you think Luigi should wave the wand and shout "Alakazam!" turn to page 18.

If you think Luigi should wave the wand and shout "Alakazook!" turn to page 104.

STOP! It's impossible to get that score. Turn back to the page you were just on and check your answer carefully.

34

"Leave everything to me," says Luigi. "I'll track down that Koopa fink, faster than six Shyguys can clog a sink."

"Spare us the poetry. Just find out how to change Daddy back," says the princess.

"Wait for me," says Toad, scampering up to Luigi. He points through the window. The bridge to Water Land is off in the distance. "I can show you where Morton Koopa lives."

Luigi waves for Toad to come along.

"I'm coming, too," Mario says. "You never know when you might run into trouble."

"Big brother," Luigi says, "can't you let someone else be a hero, just once?"

"Oh, all right," Mario agrees. "You go track down Morton Koopa. I'll just wait here and—*Achoo!*—and sneeze."

Wooster hands him a large, nose-shaped box of tissues. "Thanks," says Mario.

Luigi and Toad climb out the open window.

Starting from a berry bush near the palace, muddy three-toed footprints lead along the road toward Water Land.

The trail is easy to navigate. Not only do our heroes have Morton's footprints to follow, but the turtle has left a trail of candy wrappers along the way. The garbage-strewn road winds around brick walls, through a patch of Piranha Plants, and on toward the distant zone known as Water Land.

Solve this puzzle to find out what else Luigi will find in Water Land:

- There's a secret message in the water, but the reflection from the sign is covering it up. Hold the page up to a mirror and cross out the 18 letters in the water that also appear on the sign. The leftover letters will tell you what's in store for Luigi.

Turn to page 117.

"Come back here, Morton!" shouts Luigi, swimming after the canoe. "You've done something awful to the Mushroom King."

"I don't know." Morton chuckles. "I thought it was kind of bunny—get it? Hah, hah, hah!" He continues paddling away.

"You're not scared, are you?" asks Luigi, struggling to keep up with the canoe.

"What?" Morton stops paddling.

"A big, strong turtle like you," Luigi continues, "running away from a plumber?"

"Who's running away?" bellows Morton. He stands up in the canoe, clutching the paddle.

Luigi leaps right out of the water and makes a dive for the angry turtle.

Solve this puzzle to find out what happens next:

- Choose one of these two paths from the plumber to the turtle. Trace it with your finger or a pencil. Then read the directions below.

**If the path hits the canoe, turn to page 94.
If the path misses the canoe, turn to page 91.**

Luigi dives for the turtle, but Morton skips out of the way. *Clang!* Luigi crashes into a stack of royal ceremonial cowbells. Before he can get up, Luigi hears the patter of toenails against the marble floor. Morton slides out the window and is gone.

"A lot of help you turned out to be!" snaps Princess Toadstool. She marches into the throne room a few yards ahead of Mario and Toad and gazes around the royal chamber.

"Oh no!" she groans, examining her 400-year-old miniature tomato garden. A large, three-toed footprint is pressed into the center of the plastic basin. "Now I'm really, really, really mad! Where's Wooster?"

A tall, pale mushroom pokes his head meekly out from behind the throne. "Hello, your Highness," he whimpers.

Turn to page 37.

"I can't help you change the king back to normal," Morton tells Luigi. "That wand only works in one direction."

"We found that out," says Luigi.

"My brother Iggy can fix your king. He has a magic silver whistle that can do it," Morton continues. "But good luck getting help from him!" The turtle laughs sourly. Then he bares his fangs. "That's all I know," he snarls. "Now let me go!"

Morton seems to be telling the truth, Luigi thinks. With one foot, he pushes the turtle off the small island. Morton rights himself in the water and paddles away.

"That's that," the plumber says, wiping some slime from his boot. "Now how am I going to find Iggy?"

As the plumber scratches his head, he sees something approaching in the sky.

"Could it be the Doom Ship again?" asks

Luigi, hopefully. But the object is much too small to be the Koopas' private flying fortress. As it gets closer, Luigi makes out three familiar figures perched on a flying carpet. Soon Mario, the princess and Toad swoop down from the sky.

"Take me to Iggy Koopa," says Luigi, boarding the rug.

"That's easy," replies the princess, as she commands the magic carpet to rise back into the air. "I just saw him on the Doom Ship, heading the other way."

As the four of them sail through the sky, Luigi tells the others what Morton revealed about the magic whistle. Suddenly Toad begins to jump up and down excitedly, almost upsetting the carpet.

"Settle down!" shouts the princess over the rush of air.

"Look," says Toad, pointing to the water, far below. Luigi catches a quick glimpse of the Doom Ship. Then it disappears into a wide pipe sticking out of the water.

"Follow that boat!" Luigi shouts.

Solve this puzzle to find out where the four heroes are headed:

- The name of a place can be spelled out with the letters on these flying carpets. Start with the rug that has the smallest number of fringes on each end. Read the letters on it. Then read the letters on the rug with the next smallest number of fringes. Keep going in order, from smallest to largest. The letters spell out our heroes' destination.

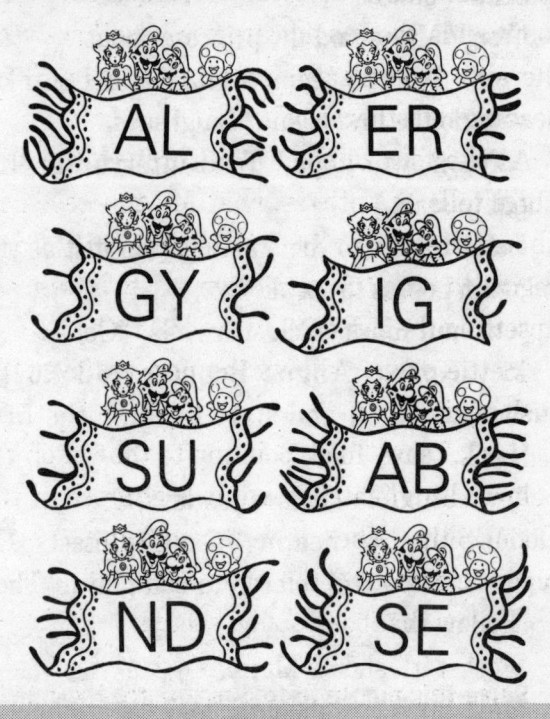

Turn to page 87.

38

"I'm going to run the obstacle course myself," Luigi announces.

"You?" Mario and the princess shout.

"Yes. I'm the team captain and I think I should do the first event," Luigi says.

"C'mon, you guys," Toad interrupts. "It's about to start."

Luigi rushes to the starting line, just as the penguin begins to speak.

"On your mark," Feldspar calls. "Get—"

Roy Koopa, Angus Boomer and Rocky Wrench take off and start to climb the first ledge.

"... set. Go!" Feldspar squawks.

"Hey, they're cheating!" Luigi protests. He walks toward the referee to complain. "They started early."

"Forget it!" shouts Mario.

"Just catch up!" the princess calls.

Luigi turns and scurries along the first part of

the course. He is much better at jumping and climbing than is the giant turtle, Angus. By the time the athletes reach the water, Luigi is in third place, with Rocky and Roy ahead of him.

ZAP! An electric jellyfish brushes against Luigi, giving him a painful jolt. Stunned, he stops paddling. Seconds later, Angus splashes past.

"Haw! Haw!" the giant turtle roars. "Wait here, and I'll get you some electric peanut butter to go with that jellyfish."

Luigi slaps himself across the face to wake up. Then, he races after the others. He climbs the vines quickly and jumps onto a carpet for the home stretch.

A few hundred yards ahead, Rocky Wrench has piloted his flying carpet directly under Roy Koopa. He takes out a pair of needle-nosed pliers and swiftly cuts a large hole in Roy's carpet. With a desperate wail, the turtle falls through and tumbles to the patch of Muncher plants below. Luckily for him, the plants refuse to eat his tough flesh, but he's out of the race.

"Now there's an idea," says Luigi. He spies Angus' flying carpet only a few feet ahead. The plumber steers his craft under Angus and uses a wrench to rip a hole in the giant turtle's carpet.

Fwomp! Angus falls right on top of Luigi, squashing him flat. The two of them drift slowly across the finish line.

"Angus Boomer wins second place," shouts the penguin referee.

"Mmmmph. Mmmm-hmmmm," mumbles Luigi from underneath the giant turtle. But the judge doesn't see or hear him.

Eventually, Angus gets up from the carpet. Mario and Princess Toadstool pick the groaning Luigi up and drag him back to their bench.

"Little brother," says Mario, "a plumber should always use his wrench for good, and never for evil."

> ***** The Royals do not get a medal for this event. *****
> **Turn to page 15.**

"The princess and I will dunk beetles," Luigi commands. "Everybody else has got to guard our bucket."

"Commence play," calls Feldspar. The two Royals dash into the diamond.

Two Firesnakes playing for the Sneaks take control of the center of the field. By turning up their flames, they blast the area with heat and light. Anyone who gets within ten feet of them is blinded.

Suddenly Roy Koopa pushes his way into the center. Wearing dark glasses, he moves easily through the tussling monsters. Grinning with glee, he grabs a Hoopster.

"Hah!" he laughs. "This is easier than stealing birthday presents from my brothers!"

A squinting Rocky Wrench produces a pot of ink from his toolbox. He smears the lenses of Roy's glasses with black goo.

"Aaargh," growls the turtle, stumbling. He

trips, falls, and drops his Hoopster.

One of the Firesnakes snatches the beetle and zooms towards the Royals' bucket. Toad tries to defend it, but the glare from the Firesnake is too bright. As Toad squints, the blazing reptile zig-zags past him. Wooster is off chasing the rabbit king. Only Mario stands between the Sneak and the goal.

Just then, the king hops by, with Wooster hot on his heels. The giant rabbit brushes against the plumber.

"*Achoo!*" Mario sneezes with such force that it extinguishes the Firesnake. Smoldering, the creature drops the Hoopster.

"Luigi, catch!" shouts Mario. He tosses the beetle to his brother. Luigi leaps over the tangle of monsters in the diamond and hands the beetle to the princess. She dunks it into the Koopas' undefended bucket.

"Yes!" She raises both arms in triumph.

Unfortunately, the Hammers have scored already. When the game is finally over, the Royals receive a second place medal.

*** The Royals get one wooden medal.***
Turn to page 47.

40

"Hang on!" shouts the princess as she sends the carpet into a steep dive. The four heroes soar into the open pipe and race down through a long, dark tunnel. Suddenly, the princess brings the carpet to a halt.

"Where did you learn to drive?" asks Mario as he gasps for breath.

"Hush!" orders the princess. "Look around."

They've landed in a cavernous room beneath the sea. Cables, pulleys and chains are strewn everywhere. Hanging fish-shaped lanterns bathe the chamber with an eerie blue light. Several hallways branch out from the area.

"What is this place?" asks the princess. Her voice echoes in the emptiness.

Odd machinery and chunks of scrap metal are stacked about the great, round room. But there's no sign of the Doom Ship or its captain.

"Come on," says Luigi, stepping off the carpet. "Let's get going."

The others follow him through the echoing corridors, peeking through several glass portholes as they go. Outside, strange sea creatures swim past, paying no attention to them at all.

Then they round a corner and see something familiar. Not pleasant—just familiar. It's a wiry, five-foot-tall turtle with purplish hair and a snaggle-toothed leer. A small silver whistle is dangling from a chain around his neck.

"Iggy Koopa," Princess Toadstool cries. "Ugh!"

Iggy scowls. "Is there a leak in one of the tunnels?" he whines. "How did all these drips get in?"

Turn to page 8.

41

"Stick with me, guys, and I'll make you proud," says Luigi.

"Oh, all right," says the princess. "Just don't disappoint us."

"Achoo!" Mario sneezes as the king brushes against him.

Luigi shakes hands with his teammates and heads on to the playing field.

Cobrat has already begun his leap. The slimy snake coils himself into the shape of a spring and bounces easily over the high bar. Then he bounces again and slides neatly through the pipe. As the crowd cheers, he flings himself across the end of the course.

"One hundred fifty Mushroom Meters!" announces Feldspar.

"Hmmm," says Luigi, adjusting his cap. "Not bad, but I can do better." He checks to make sure that his plumber's shoelaces are tied tightly. Then he gets ready to jump.

If Luigi has the pogo stick or the wings, turn to page 22.

If Luigi has both the pogo stick and the wings, turn to page 101.

If Luigi doesn't have either the pogo stick or the wings, turn to page 116.

42

Luigi lands in the water right next to the canoe. He grabs one side of the craft, tips it up, and dumps Morton Koopa overboard.

"*Glub!*" gurgles the turtle, struggling to stay afloat. Luigi grabs him by his slimy green tail and flings him ashore. Morton lands in a berry bush with a thump.

A few seconds later, as the dazed turtle sits up, Luigi is standing over him.

"Okay, okay," grumbles Morton. He tosses a ruby-tipped wand to the plumber. Then he scurries away.

"That was easy," says Luigi. He tucks the wand into one of his overalls pockets and bounces back to the palace.

Along the way, he passes a ledge with a cluster of coins stacked on top. With one leap, he grabs all seven shiny objects. "Bingo!" he shouts. Then he goes on his way.

Soon he strides into the throne room, where

Wooster is still wailing about the evil that has befallen his beloved king.

Solve this puzzle for a clue about the wand:

• Study all the wands below carefully. Count the number of stripes on each handle and the number of points on each tip. Cross out every wand that doesn't have the same number of points as stripes. The letters under the remaining wands will give you a clue about the wand Morton gave Luigi.

R I N T S O

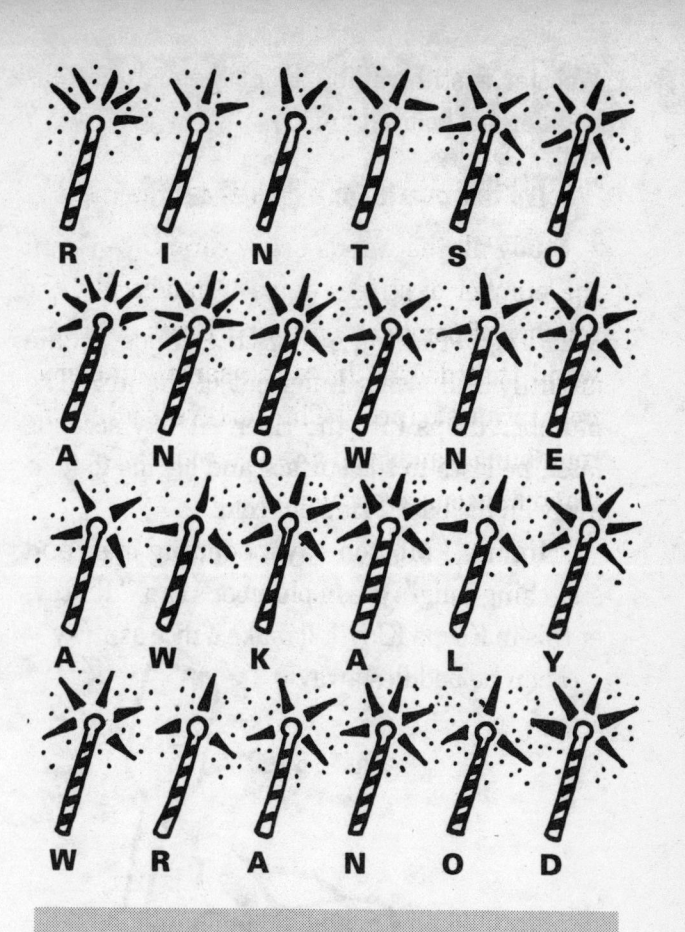

A N O W N E

A W K A L Y

W R A N O D

*** Luigi collects 7 coins. ***
*** Luigi now has the magic wand. ***
Turn to page 69.

43

*W*hump! Morton swings the canoe paddle mightily and swats Luigi out of the air. The plumber drops into the river. A few seconds later, he rises to the surface and begins to float away on his back. He's out cold!

"Hmmm," Morton says, bending over and snatching Luigi's green plumber's cap. "If I cover this in Koopa Klay, it'll make a nice ashtray."

Then he paddles away.

GAME OVER!

44

"Princess Toadstool," calls Luigi. "Go out there and make us proud!"

"Aye, Captain," replies the princess. She salutes and heads to the starting line.

"One-two-three-four-go!" Feldspar.

Even though none of them were ready, the athletes begin to climb the course. They swing, crawl, and hop from ledge to ledge. As they approach the watery part of the obstacle course, the princess is in second place, a few yards behind Rocky Wrench.

"Hey, Angus. Let me give you a hand," says Roy Koopa. He sticks one foot in the giant turtle's path.

Angus trips and hurtles forward, sailing over the other runners' heads. He lands with a tremendous belly flop in the water and lies there, stunned. Huge waves churn the water from the impact.

"Heh, heh," Roy snickers. "I guess I gave

him a foot, instead." He reaches the water in first place and paddles past the giant turtle, who is still motionless.

Close behind Rocky, Princess Toadstool splashes by, battling the waves. She continues through the water for a few yards—but then she stops suddenly. Smiling, she returns to Angus and pulls one plate from his enormous armored shell. Using the panel as a surfboard, she glides over the waves, zooms past Rocky Wrench and reaches the far side of the pool in seconds.

"Totally gnarly!" she yells, as all surfers do.

The others paddle after her desperately, but the princess's lead is now too great. She climbs the vines, hops onto a carpet, and sails gracefully over the finish line.

"The winner!" shouts Feldspar, handing her a tin first place medal.

Proudly, Princess Toadstool marches back to her teammates, who are cheering and waving from the bench.

*** The Royals get one tin medal.***
Turn to page 15.

Luigi, Mario, Princess Toadstool and Toad turn and head down the hallway. They're disappointed, but still determined. Soon they reach the large, round room where the flying carpet is parked. They climb onto the brightly colored tapestry.

"Hit it!" commands the princess.

Slowly, the carpet rises up through the opening in the ceiling. As it floats higher into the darkness, the carpet gains speed.

Soon they emerge from the great pipe's mouth, high above the surface of Water Land. Sitting cross-legged on the carpet, they look down and watch the rail-lifts and water spouts vanish in the distance. The carpet sails across the border to the Mushroom Kingdom and lands in the front yard of the palace.

Turn to page 19.

Luigi makes a flying tackle. "Gotcha!" he shouts. He grabs the turtle just before Morton reaches the open window. Both of them tumble to the throne room floor. Luigi rolls in one direction, Morton tumbles in another, and the ruby-tipped wand clatters toward the door.

The plumber and the turtle both scramble to their feet. They eye each other, then the wand and then each other again. Luigi lunges for the wand first. He grabs it and rolls head over heels to one corner of the room. "Hah!" he shouts, and holds it up triumphantly.

Snarling, Morton turns and dives out the window. Luigi races over. But it's too late.

"Rats," Luigi mutters as he stares out the window. Morton is already far away, slithering through clumps of Piranha plants. The turtle prince crosses the log bridge into Water Land, hobbles over a wall, and vanishes.

"Well, at least I have this wand. I wonder

what it's for?" Luigi says. He shrugs and shoves it into one of the pockets of his green overalls.

He notices a few coins scattered across the floor. Morton must have dropped them as he scurried out the window. "I'll keep these for later," Luigi says. "They should cover the cost of a small cheese pizza."

Just then, he hears the clatter of footsteps coming down the hall. Mario, the princess, and Toad burst into the throne room. "What's going on? Did we miss anything?" asks Mario.

"Where's Morton?" gasps Toad.

Princess Toadstool marches into the room, stepping over a broken flower pot and an empty package of royal chocolates. Her tiny pink shoes click furiously against the marble floor. Reaching the royal red carpet, she stalks up to the throne. "Where's Wooster?" she demands.

The chief mushroom assistant steps out from behind the huge wooden throne.

"He-here, your Highness," he stammers.

```
*** Luigi collects 3 coins. ***
*** Luigi now has the ruby wand. ***
         Turn to page 37.
```

Luigi steps out from behind the crate. "Let's talk turkey, turtle," he says.

"Hey!" Iggy bleats. "Who let you on board?"

"That's not important," Luigi says. "Right now, the Mushroom King is a giant rabbit."

"Tough!" snaps Iggy. He gives the Doom Ship's steering wheel a swift spin. Then he scampers to the railing and jumps. "Ta-ta," he laughs.

Iggy's white canvas backpack opens and a small parachute pops out. The turtle drifts through the clouds and disappears. Then the ship begins to spin violently out of control.

"Yikes!" Luigi lunges for the steering wheel. But it's too late. The boat flips sideways, then upside down, then rightside up again. Luigi is flung into the sky. He rockets downward as the Doom Ship spins off into the distance.

Turn to page 12.

48

Luigi dons the wings and grips his pogo stick tightly with both hands.

"Ahem." Feldspar clears his throat. "On your mark, get set, jump!"

Luigi leaps onto the pogo stick and bounces with all his might. He shoots straight up into the air, flapping his wings.

"Yaaaiieee!" he shrieks. He rockets over the high bar, over the pipe, past the end of the playing field and beyond.

"Look! He's still going!" cries the princess. Everyone gasps as Luigi streaks across the sky and vanishes in the distance.

"I guess the pogo stick and the wings were too powerful together," says Mario. "He might not land until next year."

"Disqualified!" announces Feldspar.

GAME OVER!

49

"Mario and I will defend our bucket," Luigi decides. "I want everyone else to charge down that field and score!"

The game begins. The princess and Toad scramble to the center of the diamond. Behind them, Wooster drags the king, trying to make him concentrate on the game. But the giant rabbit is more interested in nibbling the grass than in catching beetles.

With no help from their teammates, Toad and the princess are unable to get hold of any of the Hoopsters. There are just too many monsters, punching and shoving each other, trying to grab the beetles.

Cobrat slithers toward the Royals' bucket with a beetle in his fangs. "Sscore one for the Ssneakss," he hisses.

But Luigi bats the beetle away before Cobrat can dunk it. Mario grabs Cobrat's tail and whirls the snake over his head. "Back you go!"

shouts Mario, and flings Cobrat back into the center of the diamond.

Then Wendy and Roy Koopa charge at the plumbers. Roy moves in ahead of his sister. His hand is raised, as if he's about to slam something into the bucket.

"Drop that beetle!" shouts Mario, jumping in front of the charging reptile.

But it turns out not to be a beetle. Roy is clutching an orange paper bag filled with banana peels, moldy bread and a lot of other unidentifiable sticky, smelly garbage.

"Have some gross-eries!" snorts Roy Koopa. He dumps the bag over Mario's head.

While Mario wipes away egg shells and rotten cheese, Wendy Koopa slips by him and Luigi. She dunks a Hoopster into the Royals' bucket. Then Rocky Wrench and Angus Boomer race by. They dunk their Hoopsters, too.

"Game over!" shouts Feldspar.

Tired, defeated and—in Mario's case—smelly, the Royals walk back to their bench.

*** **The Royals do not get a medal for this event.** ***

Turn to page 47.

"Alakazook!" Luigi shouts, dramatically waving the ruby wand. A bolt of blazing red light flashes from the wand, and an explosion shakes the room. A cloud of dense black smoke rolls over the rabbit king, covering him completely.

"Achoo! Achoo! Ah-*achoo!*" Mario's sneezing is out of control.

Then, slowly, the smoke begins to clear. A giant, eight-foot-tall rabbit stands next to Wooster.

"Hmmm," Luigi says. He twists the wooden wand handle between his fingers, studying it. "It must be a one-way wand."

The king lifts a giant, furry paw, and starts to scratch one of his enormous floppy white ears. His golden crown rolls clanking across the throne room floor. The scratching stirs up a strong breeze in the throne room.

"What do we do now?" asks the princess in a despairing voice. She holds on to her crown with one hand to keep it from blowing off her head.

"Maybe I should try the wand again," suggests Luigi.

"Don't be a dumb plumber," snaps Mario. "We've got to track down Morton Koopa and make him change the king back."

At that, the king stops scratching his ear. The breeze dies down.

Mario tries to grab the wand from his brother. But Luigi skips to one side. He likes being in control for a change.

"Come on, Luigi," Mario says, getting frustrated. "Either zap the king again, or let's get out of here." He rubs his itchy, watery eyes. "But hurry up—my allergies are killing me!"

If you think Luigi should head out to find Morton Koopa, turn to page 73.

If you think Luigi should use the ruby wand on the king again, turn to page 119.

51

Luigi heads into the tunnel that leads away from the room where the Doom Ship landed. But before he travels far, he notices a small hinged lid bolted to the floor of the corridor.

"Hmmmm," says Luigi, lifting it open. To his delight, he finds a small compartment below the floor, completely filled with coins. "Jackpot!" he shouts, filling his pockets. "This should cover the cost of a new left-handed power monkey wrench!" Then he flips the lid shut and continues on his way down the hall.

Solve this puzzle to find out how many coins Luigi picks up:

- Choose any box with the letter A at the top. Count the coins that are in that box. Write down your total.
- Next, read the letter at the bottom of the box. Choose a new box with that letter above it. Add the coins in the new box to your total.

• Continue until you reach a box that has an X at the bottom. When that happens, you're finished. Luigi can't collect any more coins.

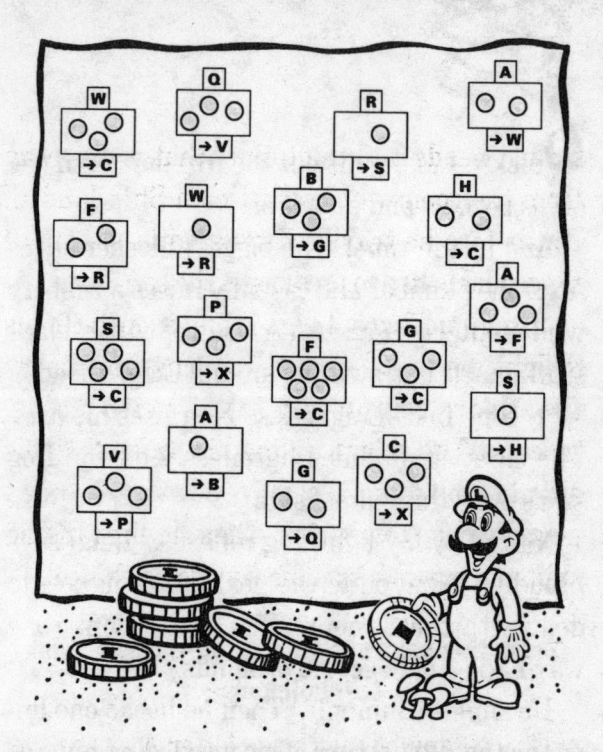

*** Luigi collects that many coins. ***

If Luigi found more than 15 coins—
turn to page 72.

If Luigi found 15 coins or less—
turn to page 33.

52

Quickly, Luigi pulls out the frog suit from one of his pockets and puts it on.

And just in time! The biggest Bloober sidles up to the plumber and casually raises a rubbery white tentacle. *Pzzzztt!* A cloud of bluish-black stuff squirts out, swirling around Luigi's head.

"Sleepy Ink!" Luigi cries. He raises his arm. The slimy stuff slides harmlessly off the frog suit's everything-proof skin.

"Saved by my lightning reflexes," Luigi says proudly. "Now, on to the next problem: how to deal with these monsters? There's only one way I know of to get rid of squids."

He smiles cunningly. Then he hooks one finger on the right corner of his mouth and pulls as hard as he can. With his other hand, he tugs at his left ear, twisting his head into a very strange shape. Next, he opens his eyes wide and stares at the bobbing Bloobers, who are watching him intently. "Ooga-booga!" he yells.

The slimy creatures panic. They swirl around the pool in terror, bumping into each other like soggy loaves of bread. Carefully dodging the frantic Bloobers, Luigi swims up to the edge of the pool and climbs out.

As the rubbery monsters swirl off to the far end of the tank, one of the Bloobers drops something.

Luigi jumps into the water and grabs the object before it sinks to the bottom. It's a shiny metal pogo stick.

"Interesting," says Luigi. He shakes the water from the pogo stick and shoves it into one of his larger pockets. "You never know when this might come in handy."

He climbs the ladder up to the hatch and out of the room.

Luigi now has a pogo stick.
Turn to page 106.

"That rotten Koopa turtle was here a few minutes ago," Luigi says. "He couldn't have gotten far. I'll get that magic wand!" Without waiting for a reply, Luigi dashes out of the throne room, down the long main hall and out into the kingdom.

Sure enough, Morton is nearby. Luigi spots him by the bank of a stream just as the turtle is climbing into a rusty metal canoe.

"Come back here, you fiend!" Luigi shouts, dashing towards Morton.

"Not on your life, plumber," Morton snarls. He begins to paddle away, down the winding stream. Luigi dives into the water after him.

If Luigi has the anchor, turn to page 50.
If Luigi doesn't have the anchor, turn to page 76.

54

"The first event is the obstacle course," squawks the penguin as horns blare. All heads turn toward an area just north of the stadium.

The first third of the course is a series of ledges, blocks and stairs. Some are made of bricks, some are made of wood and others are made of shiny metal. They're packed close together in steep pyramids with sudden drop-offs. Then a long, narrow waterway begins. Luigi can see many nasty creatures swimming about in the depths. As he gazes over the pool, he spots an electric jellyfish bobbing on the surface.

At the far end of the water, several vines climb high into the air, where a fleet of magic carpets are parked. The last part of the course is a flying race to the finish line, with hungry Muncher plants waiting eagerly below.

"Roy Koopa will be competing for the Koopa team," announces Feldspar.

A big, burly turtle in pink sunglasses steps

forward. "I hope I'm running against you," he growls to Mario as he trudges past. "I've still got bruises from the last time we met. I'd like to settle the score."

Mario smiles, but says nothing.

"For the Hammer team: Angus Boomer!" the penguin referee shouts. Some of the smaller mushrooms in the stands shrink back nervously as a huge shadow drifts over them. An enormous, armored turtle lumbers past.

"Rocky Wrench will run for the Sneaks," says Feldspar. A big rodent carrying a toolbox hops by the Royals' bench.

The princess wrinkles her nose. "That handbag does not go with that outfit," she says.

"Nice wrenches, though," Mario comments.

"All right," says Luigi. "I've given a lot of thought to who should run this course for our team, and I've made up my mind. . . ."

Solve this puzzle for a clue:

• Study the trails from the princess, Mario and Luigi to the stadium. The only unbroken trail that reaches the stadium belongs to the person who should run the obstacle course.

If you think Luigi should ask Mario to run the obstacle course, turn to page 24.

If you think Luigi should ask the princess to run the obstacle course, turn to page 95.

If you think Luigi should run the course himself, turn to page 82.

55

"Better stay put for a while and see what gives," thinks Luigi. He remains hidden behind the stack of wooden crates, peeking out at Iggy Koopa every few minutes. The turtle guides the Doom Ship by its wooden steering wheel while humming a tune—badly.

The Doom Ship sails through the clouds for what seems like hours, traveling deep into the heart of Water Land. Suddenly, the ship lurches forward and heads straight down toward the water.

"What's happening?" Luigi blurts out as he falls against the rail. He grips the Doom Ship's rail tightly and peeks over the side.

"Yikes!" he cries. The bow of the ship is about to smash into the water!

Solve this puzzle for a clue:

- Study this outline of the Doom Ship carefully. Then read all the letters in the box that are inside outlines that are exactly the same shape. Those letters will help you decide what Luigi should do next.

> **If you think Luigi should jump off the ship quickly, turn to page 12.**
>
> **If you think he should hang on and stay hidden, turn to page 41.**

56

Luigi leaps over the high bar and dives through the wide green pipe. But by the time he reaches the third part of the jump, he's exhausted. He jumps as far as he can and hits the ground at the 30-Mushroom-Meter mark.

"That's not too bad a jump," Luigi tells himself. Then he looks up as Iggy Koopa sails high over his head. The evil turtle uses a rocket-powered booster and lands at the 160-Mushroom-Meter mark.

"Hee, hee," says Iggy, and walks back to the Koopas' bench.

Feldspar hands Luigi a chocolate, third place medal and sends him back to his bench to tally up the Royals' final score.

*** **The Royals get one chocolate medal.** ***
Turn to page 57.

57

As soon as Luigi and Toad cross the bridge into Water Land, the trees and valleys of the Mushroom Kingdom vanish. There's water as far as the eye can see, dotted with islands that are linked by rickety wooden bridges.

In the Mushroom Kingdom, Luigi often has to battle Koopa Troopas or Goomba mushrooms. There are none of those here. Instead, the air is full of Cheep Cheeps—vicious flying fish with crab-like claws.

"Look over there!" Toad cries excitedly. As he bats away a Cheep Cheep, he points to a small, square object in the distance. It looks like a box, floating on the water.

"Let's check it out," says Luigi. They head off toward the odd, bobbing object.

As they travel deeper into Water Land, however, the bridges become less frequent. Luigi and Toad must jump from one island to another. After a while, the islands start to get farther apart—and the Cheep Cheeps start to get bigger. One of them zooms up to Toad.

"Ouch!" yelps the royal mushroom retainer, when the owl-faced Cheep Cheep nips him on the ear. "I can't take this anymore."

"Okay, little friend," says Luigi. "You go back to the others. I'll be all right."

Toad scrambles to safety, and Luigi goes on alone. He jumps over a waterspout and dodges a swarm of leaping Bloober squids. He also picks up some coins that are scattered on a small, sandy island. "Someone must have dropped these before the Cheep Cheeps got him," muses Luigi.

Soon the strange object is a few yards away. "It's a boat," Luigi observes. Tied to an island is a houseboat. The water around it is black. Bags of garbage bob everywhere.

"I do believe I detect the faint odor of Koopas in the air," says Luigi. He sniffs once. Then he coughs. "On second thought, maybe it's not so faint," he wheezes.

*** **Luigi collects 6 coins.** ***
Turn to page 58.

58

Luigi decides to use the wand a second time. "Alakazook!" he shouts.

Once again, a ruby light flashes from the wand, followed by a cloud of red smoke. But this time, the silence is torn by the sound of splintering glass.

"Eek!" shouts the princess.

"Aaaiieee!" Toad shrieks in terror. He dashes through the open double doors and disappears down the grand hallway, screaming.

Luigi looks up—then up, and up, and up! The throne room is filled by a sixty-four-foot-tall rabbit! His head has broken through the crystal ceiling of the throne room. His floppy ears look like two enormous white flags, waving high above the palace.

"He's chewing on the royal chimney!" Wooster wails. The chief mushroom assistant jumps up and down between two of the king's humongous toes. "And look," he shrieks, "the royal carpets have been ruined!"

"Oops," Luigi says. He drops the wand on the ground. "Maybe I am the dumber plumber. What a bummer."

Then, the king begins to shift his weight from one massive hind leg to the other. Slowly he steps forward. Luigi looks up in time to see a massive fuzzy foot coming down upon him and his friends.

"That's a bigger bummer," he sighs. . . .

GAME OVER!

Drip by Drip Scorecard

Circle each object as you collect it.

Keep track of your coins here:

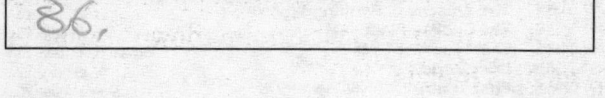

86,

Now, use this chart to find out your P. P. R. (Personal Plumber Rating) for this adventure. Just score 10 points for every coin that Luigi has at the end of the story. Then look up your rating on the chart.

Did you defeat Morton Koopa? Did you swim with the Bloobers? Read the book again, until you reach the highest score possible.

Rating	Score
Mushroom Games Champ and Master Plumber	801 or more
Drain Chief —Two Plumbs Up	601 to 800
Major League Faucet-Fixer	401 to 600
Minor League Faucet-Fixer	201 to 400
Monkey with a Wrench	200 or less

A Selected List of Fiction from Mammoth

While every effort is made to keep prices low, it is sometimes necessary to increase prices at short notice. Mandarin Paperbacks reserves the right to show new retail prices on covers which may differ from those previously advertised in the text or elsewhere.

The prices shown below were correct at the time of going to press.

☐	7497 0978 2	**Trial of Anna Cotman**	Vivien Alcock £2.50
☐	7497 0712 7	**Under the Enchanter**	Nina Beachcroft £2.50
☐	7497 0106 4	**Rescuing Gloria**	Gillian Cross £2.50
☐	7497 0035 1	**The Animals of Farthing Wood**	Colin Dann £3.50
☐	7497 0613 9	**The Cuckoo Plant**	Adam Ford £3.50
☐	7497 0443 8	**Fast From the Gate**	Michael Hardcastle £1.99
☐	7497 0136 6	**I Am David**	Anne Holm £2.99
☐	7497 0295 8	**First Term**	Mary Hooper £2.99
☐	7497 0033 5	**Lives of Christopher Chant**	Diana Wynne Jones £2.99
☐	7497 0601 5	**The Revenge of Samuel Stokes**	Penelope Lively £2.99
☐	7497 0344 X	**The Haunting**	Margaret Mahy £2.99
☐	7497 0537 X	**Why The Whales Came**	Michael Morpurgo £2.99
☐	7497 0831 X	**The Snow Spider**	Jenny Nimmo £2.99
☐	7497 0992 8	**My Friend Flicka**	Mary O'Hara £2.99
☐	7497 0525 6	**The Message**	Judith O'Neill £2.99
☐	7497 0410 1	**Space Demons**	Gillian Rubinstein £2.50
☐	7497 0151 X	**The Flawed Glass**	Ian Strachan £2.99

All these books are available at your bookshop or newsagent, or can be ordered direct from the publisher. Just tick the titles you want and fill in the form below.

Mandarin Paperbacks, Cash Sales Department, PO Box 11, Falmouth, Cornwall TR10 9EN.

Please send cheque or postal order, no currency, for purchase price quoted and allow the following for postage and packing:

UK including BFPO   £1.00 for the first book, 50p for the second and 30p for each additional book ordered to a maximum charge of £3.00.

Overseas including Eire   £2 for the first book, £1.00 for the second and 50p for each additional book thereafter.

NAME (Block letters) ....

ADDRESS ....

....

☐ I enclose my remittance for ....

☐ I wish to pay by Access/Visa Card Number

Expiry Date